WELCC

TRAVEL
AUSTRALIA
BY VAN
PLANNER & DIARY

MW00873911

THIS JOURNAL BELONGS TO:

INSIDE...
- Map and Visual Planner
- Trip-at-a-glance Planner
- Bucket List
- Trip Budget Planner
- Itinerary Details - Flights, Accommodation and Transfers
- 5-week day planner
- Packing List Generator
- Common Conversions
- Winter and Summer Time Zones
- Fuel and Expense Logs
- Reversible 32-day Journal

If found, please return to:

_____

_____

_____

AUSTRALIA BY VAN

VISUAL PLANNER

Timor Sea

INDIAN OCEAN

Bathurst

Darwin

Kakadu National Park

Mindi Beach

Arnhem Land

Barkly Tableland

Collier Bay

Kimberley Plateau

How to use...
List your personal places of interest in the box, then draw a line to the area
...like this!
Rottnest Island

Broome

Tanami Desert

NORTHERN TERRITORY

Barrow

Great Sandy Desert

Tropic of Capricorn

Alice Springs

Macdonnell Ranges

Gibson Desert

Uluru

WESTERN AUSTRALIA

Barrow Range

Great Victoria Desert

SOUTH AUSTRALIA

The Pinnacles

Nambung National Park

Nullabor Plain

KEY

▬▬	Road
──	Railway
─ ─ ─	State Border
●	National Park
●	Point of Interest
○	Major City
⊕	Major Airport
⚓	Seaport

Perth

Kings Park

Great Australian Bight

Kangaroo Island

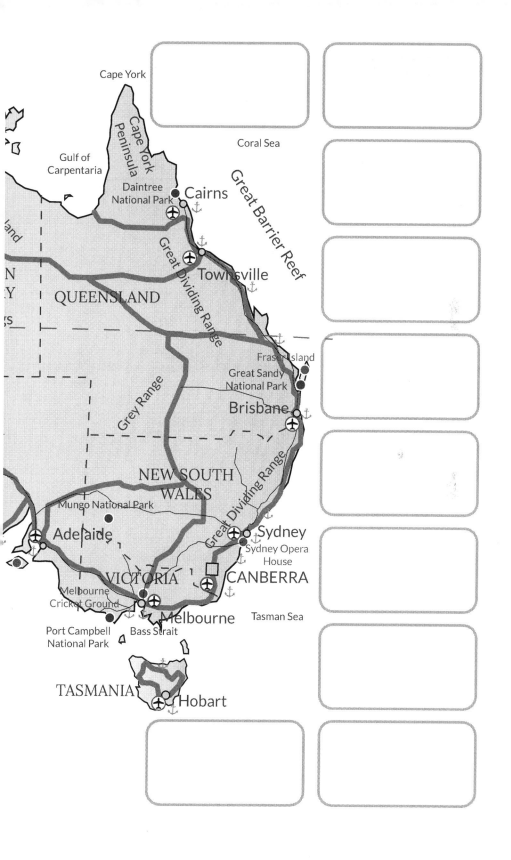

AUSTRALIA BY VAN

TRIP AT A GLANCE

Where:

When:

Who:

What:

Why:

How:

AUSTRALIA BY VAN

BUCKET LIST

Area: _____

Essential: _____

_____

_____

_____

_____

_____

_____

_____

_____

_____

_____

_____

Nice to do: _____

_____

_____

_____

_____

_____

_____

...if we have time: _____

_____

_____

_____

AUSTRALIA BY VAN

BUCKET LIST

Area: _____

Essential:
_____
_____
_____
_____
_____
_____
_____
_____
_____
_____
_____
_____

Nice to do:
_____
_____
_____
_____
_____
_____
_____

...if we have time:
_____
_____
_____

AUSTRALIA BY VAN

BUCKET LIST

Area: _____

Essential: _____

_____
_____
_____
_____
_____
_____
_____
_____
_____
_____
_____
_____

Nice to do: _____

_____
_____
_____
_____
_____
_____

...if we have time: _____

_____
_____
_____

AUSTRALIA BY VAN
BUCKET LIST

Area:
_____

Essential:
_____
_____
_____
_____
_____
_____
_____
_____
_____
_____
_____
_____
_____

Nice to do:
_____
_____
_____
_____
_____
_____
_____
_____

...if we have time:
_____
_____
_____

AUSTRALIA BY VAN

BUCKET LIST

Area:

Essential:

Nice to do:

...if we have time:

AUSTRALIA BY VAN

TRIP BUDGET

Currency: _____

Expense	Budget	Actual	Notes
TRANSPORT			
Airfares			
Car Hire			
Gas/Fuel			
Fares			
Misc			
OTHER			
Visas			
Insurance			
Phone/Sim Card			
ACCOMMODATION			
Hotels/Hostels			
BnB's			
Campsites			
Misc			
SIGHTS & ACTIVITIES			
Tickets			
Total page 1			

AUSTRALIA BY VAN
TRIP BUDGET

Currency:

Expense	Budget	Actual	Notes
SHOPPING *buy here*			
Luggage			
Apps			
Maps/Guides			
SHOPPING *buy there*			
Souvenirs			
Clothes			
Tax-Free			
Misc			
FOOD & DRINK			
Snacks/Bottled Drinks			
Breakfasts			
Lunches			
Dinners			
Groceries			
Bar/Pub			
Misc			
Total page 2			
Total page 1			
TOTAL			

AUSTRALIA BY VAN
ITINERARY

Dates:

TRANSFER

Company:

Address:

Phone: Confirmation #

Notes:

FLIGHT

Airline: Flight #

Location: Reference #

Check in Time: Departure Time:

Notes:

CAR HIRE/TRANSFER

Company:

Address:

Phone: Confirmation #

Notes

ACCOMMODATION

Name of Hotel:

Address:

Phone: Confirmation #

Notes:

AUSTRALIA BY VAN

ITINERARY

Dates:

TRANSFER

Company:

Address:

Phone: Confirmation #

Notes:

FLIGHT

Airline: Flight #

Location: Reference #

Check in Time: Departure Time:

Notes:

CAR HIRE/TRANSFER

Company:

Address:

Phone: Confirmation #

Notes

ACCOMMODATION

Name of Hotel:

Address:

Phone: Confirmation #

Notes:

AUSTRALIA BY VAN

ITINERARY

Dates:

TRANSFER

Company:

Address:

Phone: Confirmation #

Notes:

FLIGHT

Airline: Flight #

Location: Reference #

Check in Time: Departure Time:

Notes:

CAR HIRE/TRANSFER

Company:

Address:

Phone: Confirmation #

Notes

ACCOMMODATION

Name of Hotel:

Address:

Phone: Confirmation #

Notes:

AUSTRALIA BY VAN

ITINERARY

Dates:

TRANSFER

Company:

Address:

Phone: Confirmation #

Notes:

FLIGHT

Airline: Flight #

Location: Reference #

Check in Time: Departure Time:

Notes:

CAR HIRE/TRANSFER

Company:

Address:

Phone: Confirmation #

Notes

ACCOMMODATION

Name of Hotel:

Address:

Phone: Confirmation #

Notes:

AUSTRALIA BY VAN

ITINERARY

Dates: _____

TRANSFER

Company: _____

Address: _____

_____

Phone: _____ Confirmation # _____

Notes: _____

FLIGHT

Airline: _____ Flight # _____

Location: _____ Reference # _____

Check in Time: _____ Departure Time: _____

Notes: _____

CAR HIRE/TRANSFER

Company: _____

Address: _____

_____

Phone: _____ Confirmation # _____

Notes _____

ACCOMMODATION

Name of Hotel: _____

Address: _____

_____

Phone: _____ Confirmation # _____

Notes: _____

AUSTRALIA BY VAN
ITINERARY

Dates: _____

TRANSFER

Company: _____

Address: _____

_____

Phone: _____ Confirmation # _____

Notes: _____

FLIGHT

Airline: _____ Flight # _____

Location: _____ Reference # _____

Check in Time: _____ Departure Time: _____

Notes: _____

CAR HIRE/TRANSFER

Company: _____

Address: _____

_____

Phone: _____ Confirmation # _____

Notes _____

ACCOMMODATION

Name of Hotel: _____

Address: _____

_____

Phone: _____ Confirmation # _____

Notes: _____

AUSTRALIA BY VAN

ITINERARY

Dates:

TRANSFER

Company:

Address:

Phone: Confirmation #

Notes:

FLIGHT

Airline: Flight #

Location: Reference #

Check in Time: Departure Time:

Notes:

CAR HIRE/TRANSFER

Company:

Address:

Phone: Confirmation #

Notes

ACCOMMODATION

Name of Hotel:

Address:

Phone: Confirmation #

Notes:

AUSTRALIA BY VAN

ITINERARY

Dates: _____

TRANSFER

Company: _____

Address: _____

_____

Phone: _____ Confirmation # _____

Notes: _____

FLIGHT

Airline: _____ Flight # _____

Location: _____ Reference # _____

Check in Time: _____ Departure Time: _____

Notes: _____

CAR HIRE/TRANSFER

Company: _____

Address: _____

_____

Phone: _____ Confirmation # _____

Notes _____

ACCOMMODATION

Name of Hotel: _____

Address: _____

_____

Phone: _____ Confirmation # _____

Notes: _____

AUSTRALIA BY VAN

DAY PLANNER

PRIORITY	MONDAY	TUESDAY	WEDNESDAY

AUSTRALIA BY VAN

DAY PLANNER

THURSDAY	FRIDAY	SATURDAY	SUNDAY

AUSTRALIA BY VAN

DAY PLANNER

PRIORITY	MONDAY	TUESDAY	WEDNESDAY

_____

_____

AUSTRALIA BY VAN

DAY PLANNER

THURSDAY	FRIDAY	SATURDAY	SUNDAY

AUSTRALIA BY VAN

DAY PLANNER

PRIORITY	MONDAY	TUESDAY	WEDNESDAY

AUSTRALIA BY VAN

DAY PLANNER

THURSDAY	FRIDAY	SATURDAY	SUNDAY

_____

_____

AUSTRALIA BY VAN

DAY PLANNER

PRIORITY	MONDAY	TUESDAY	WEDNESDAY

AUSTRALIA BY VAN

DAY PLANNER

THURSDAY	FRIDAY	SATURDAY	SUNDAY

_____

_____

_____

AUSTRALIA BY VAN
PACKING LIST

CLOTHING	
Basics	**Casual**
☐	☐
☐	☐
☐	☐
☐	☐
☐	☐
☐	☐
☐	☐
Dressy	**Outerwear**
☐	☐
☐	☐
☐	☐
☐	☐
☐	☐
☐	☐
☐	☐
Accessories	**Wearing**
☐	☐
☐	☐
☐	☐
☐	☐
☐	☐

AUSTRALIA BY VAN

PACKING LIST

Toiletries	Medication
☐	☐
☐	☐
☐	☐
☐	☐
☐	☐

Tech/Gear	Entertainment
☐	☐
☐	☐
☐	☐
☐	☐
☐	☐

Other	Food/Snacks
☐	☐
☐	☐
☐	☐
☐	☐

Travel Docs	Carry On
☐	☐
☐	☐
☐	☐
☐	☐
☐	☐

AUSTRALIA BY VAN
CONVERSIONS

Date:

LENGTH

1 centimetre (cm)	=	10 millimetres (mm)
1 inch	=	2.54 centimetres (cm)
1 foot	=	0.3048 metres (m)
1 foot	=	12 inches
1 yard	=	3 feet
1 metre (m)	=	100 centimetres (cm)
1 metre (m)	=	3.280839895 feet
1 furlong	=	660 feet
1 kilometre (km)	=	1000 metres (m)
1 kilometre (km)	=	0.62137119 miles
1 mile	=	5280 ft
1 mile	=	1.609344 kilometres (km)
1 nautical mile	=	1.852 kilometres (km)

WEIGHT

1 milligram (mg)	=	0.001 grams (g)
1 gram (g)	=	0.001 kilograms (kg)
1 gram (g)	=	0.035273962 ounces
1 ounce	=	28.34952312 grams (g)
1 ounce	=	0.0625 pounds
1 pound (lb)	=	16 ounces
1 pound (lb)	=	0.45359237 kilograms (kg)
1 kilogram (kg)	=	1000 grams
1 kilogram (kg)	=	35.273962 ounces
1 kilogram (kg)	=	2.20462262 pounds (lb)
1 stone	=	14 pounds
1 short ton	=	2000 pounds
1 metric ton	=	1000 kilograms (kg)

AREA

1 square foot	=	144 square inches
1 square foot	=	929.0304 sq centimetres
1 square yard	=	9 square feet
1 square metre	=	10.7639104 square feet
1 acre	=	43,560 square feet
1 hectare	=	10,000 square metres
1 hectare	=	2.4710538 acres
1 sq kilometre	=	100 hectares
1 sq mile	=	2.58998811 sq kilometres
1 sq mile	=	640 acres

SPEED

1 mph	=	1.46666667 fps
1 mph	=	1.609344 kph
1 knot	=	1.150779448 mph
1 foot per second	=	0.68181818 mph (mph)
1 kph	=	0.62137119 mph

VOLUME

1 US tablespoon	=	3 US teaspoons
1 US fluid ounce	=	29.57353 milliliters (ml)
1 US cup	=	16 US tablespoons
1 US cup	=	8 US fluid ounces
1 US pint	=	2 US cups
1 US pint	=	16 US fluid ounces
1 litre (l)	=	33.8140227 US fl ounces
1 litre (l)	=	1000 milliliters (ml)
1 US quart	=	2 US pints
1 US gallon	=	4 US quarts
1 US gallon	=	3.78541178 litres

TEMPERATURE

Fahrenheit / **Celcius**

Fahrenheit	Celcius
130	55
120	50
110	45
100	40
90	35
80	30
70	25
60	20
50	15
40	10
30	5
20	0
10	-5
0	-10
-10	-15
-20	-20
-30	-25
	-30
	-35

AUSTRALIA BY VAN

ITINERARY

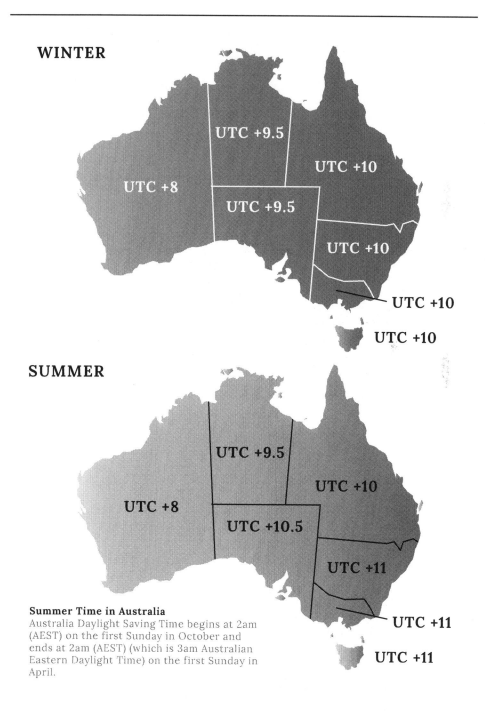

WINTER

UTC +9.5

UTC +10

UTC +8

UTC +9.5

UTC +10

UTC +10

UTC +10

SUMMER

UTC +9.5

UTC +10

UTC +8

UTC +10.5

UTC +11

UTC +11

UTC +11

Summer Time in Australia
Australia Daylight Saving Time begins at 2am
(AEST) on the first Sunday in October and
ends at 2am (AEST) (which is 3am Australian
Eastern Daylight Time) on the first Sunday in
April.

AUSTRALIA BY VAN

EXPENSE LOG

Currency:

Date	Vendor	Description	Amount

AUSTRALIA BY VAN

FUEL LOG

Currency:

Date	Odometer	Litres	Cost

AUSTRALIA BY VAN

PRE-TRAVEL CHECKLIST

1-MONTH BEFORE

- [ ]
- [ ]
- [ ]
- [ ]
- [ ]
- [ ]

2-WEEKS BEFORE

- [ ]
- [ ]
- [ ]
- [ ]
- [ ]
- [ ]

1-WEEK BEFORE

- [ ]
- [ ]
- [ ]
- [ ]
- [ ]
- [ ]

2-DAYS BEFORE

- [ ]
- [ ]
- [ ]
- [ ]
- [ ]
- [ ]

24-HOURS BEFORE

- [ ]
- [ ]
- [ ]
- [ ]
- [ ]
- [ ]

DAY OF TRAVEL

- [ ]
- [ ]
- [ ]
- [ ]
- [ ]
- [ ]

AUSTRALIA BY VAN
BUCKET LIST

BON VOYAGE!

NOW, TURN THE PLANNER OVER AND
RECORD YOUR JOURNEY IN THE 32-DAY JOURNAL

AUSTRALIA BY VAN

TRAVEL DIARY

Date:

AUSTRALIA BY VAN

TRAVEL DIARY

Date:

SCHEDULE	SITESEEING
9:00	
9:30	
10:00	
10:30	
11:00	
11:30	
12:00	
12:30	WEATHER
1:00	
1:30	
2:00	
2:30	SPENDING MONEY
3:00	
3:30	
4:00	
4:30	NOTES
5:00	
5:30	

SPENDING MONEY

BUDGET	SPENT	REMAINING

EAT

B	
L	
D	

AUSTRALIA BY VAN

TRAVEL DIARY

Date:

AUSTRALIA BY VAN

TRAVEL DIARY

Date:

SCHEDULE	SITESEEING
9:00	
9:30	
10:00	
10:30	
11:00	
11:30	
12:00	
12:30	**WEATHER**
1:00	
1:30	
2:00	
2:30	**SPENDING MONEY**

BUDGET	SPENT	REMAINING

SCHEDULE	
3:00	
3:30	
4:00	
4:30	**NOTES**
5:00	
5:30	

EAT

B	
L	
D	

AUSTRALIA BY VAN

TRAVEL DIARY

Date:

AUSTRALIA BY VAN

TRAVEL DIARY

Date:

SCHEDULE	SITESEEING
9:00	
9:30	
10:00	
10:30	
11:00	
11:30	
12:00	
12:30	**WEATHER**
1:00	
1:30	
2:00	
2:30	**SPENDING MONEY**

BUDGET	SPENT	REMAINING

3:00
3:30
4:00

NOTES

4:30
5:00
5:30

EAT

B	
L	
D	

AUSTRALIA BY VAN

TRAVEL DIARY

Date:

AUSTRALIA BY VAN

TRAVEL DIARY

Date:

SCHEDULE	SITESEEING
9:00	
9:30	
10:00	
10:30	
11:00	
11:30	
12:00	
12:30	**WEATHER**
1:00	
1:30	
2:00	
2:30	**SPENDING MONEY**
3:00	BUDGET / SPENT / REMAINING
3:30	
4:00	
4:30	**NOTES**
5:00	
5:30	

EAT

B	
L	
D	

AUSTRALIA BY VAN
TRAVEL DIARY

Date:

AUSTRALIA BY VAN

TRAVEL DIARY

Date:

SCHEDULE	SITESEEING
9:00	
9:30	
10:00	
10:30	
11:00	
11:30	
12:00	
12:30	**WEATHER**
1:00	
1:30	
2:00	
2:30	**SPENDING MONEY**
3:00	
3:30	
4:00	
4:30	**NOTES**
5:00	
5:30	

SPENDING MONEY

BUDGET	SPENT	REMAINING

EAT

B	
L	
D	

AUSTRALIA BY VAN
TRAVEL DIARY

Date:

AUSTRALIA BY VAN

TRAVEL DIARY

Date:

SCHEDULE	SITESEEING
9:00	
9:30	
10:00	
10:30	
11:00	
11:30	
12:00	
12:30	**WEATHER**
1:00	
1:30	
2:00	
2:30	**SPENDING MONEY**
3:00	BUDGET / SPENT / REMAINING
3:30	
4:00	
4:30	**NOTES**
5:00	
5:30	

EAT

B	
L	
D	

AUSTRALIA BY VAN
TRAVEL DIARY

Date:

AUSTRALIA BY VAN

TRAVEL DIARY

Date:

SCHEDULE	SITESEEING
9:00	
9:30	
10:00	
10:30	
11:00	
11:30	
12:00	
12:30	**WEATHER**
1:00	
1:30	
2:00	
2:30	**SPENDING MONEY**
3:00	
3:30	
4:00	
4:30	**NOTES**
5:00	
5:30	

SPENDING MONEY

BUDGET	SPENT	REMAINING

EAT

B	
L	
D	

AUSTRALIA BY VAN

TRAVEL DIARY

Date:

AUSTRALIA BY VAN

TRAVEL DIARY

Date:

SCHEDULE	SITESEEING
9:00	
9:30	
10:00	
10:30	
11:00	
11:30	
12:00	
12:30	**WEATHER**
1:00	
1:30	
2:00	
2:30	**SPENDING MONEY**

BUDGET	SPENT	REMAINING

SCHEDULE	
3:00	
3:30	
4:00	
4:30	**NOTES**
5:00	
5:30	

EAT

B	
L	
D	

AUSTRALIA BY VAN

TRAVEL DIARY

Date:

AUSTRALIA BY VAN

TRAVEL DIARY

Date:

SCHEDULE	SITESEEING
9:00	
9:30	
10:00	
10:30	
11:00	
11:30	
12:00	
12:30	**WEATHER**
1:00	
1:30	
2:00	
2:30	**SPENDING MONEY**
3:00	BUDGET / SPENT / REMAINING
3:30	
4:00	
4:30	**NOTES**
5:00	
5:30	

EAT

B	
L	
D	

AUSTRALIA BY VAN
TRAVEL DIARY

Date:

AUSTRALIA BY VAN

TRAVEL DIARY

Date:

SCHEDULE	SITESEEING
9:00	
9:30	
10:00	
10:30	
11:00	
11:30	
12:00	
12:30	WEATHER
1:00	
1:30	
2:00	
2:30	SPENDING MONEY
3:00	BUDGET / SPENT / REMAINING
3:30	
4:00	
4:30	NOTES
5:00	
5:30	

EAT

B	
L	
D	

AUSTRALIA BY VAN
TRAVEL DIARY

Date:

AUSTRALIA BY VAN

TRAVEL DIARY

Date:

SCHEDULE	SITESEEING

9:00

9:30

10:00

10:30

11:00

11:30

12:00

12:30 — **WEATHER**

1:00

1:30

2:00

2:30 — **SPENDING MONEY**

BUDGET	SPENT	REMAINING

3:00

3:30

4:00

4:30 — **NOTES**

5:00

5:30

EAT

B	
L	
D	

AUSTRALIA BY VAN

TRAVEL DIARY

Date:

AUSTRALIA BY VAN

TRAVEL DIARY

Date:

SCHEDULE	SITESEEING
9:00	
9:30	
10:00	
10:30	
11:00	
11:30	
12:00	
12:30	**WEATHER**
1:00	
1:30	
2:00	
2:30	**SPENDING MONEY**
3:00	BUDGET / SPENT / REMAINING
3:30	
4:00	
4:30	**NOTES**
5:00	
5:30	

EAT

B

L

D

AUSTRALIA BY VAN
TRAVEL DIARY

Date:

AUSTRALIA BY VAN

TRAVEL DIARY

Date:

SCHEDULE	SITESEEING
9:00	
9:30	
10:00	
10:30	
11:00	
11:30	
12:00	
12:30	**WEATHER**
1:00	
1:30	
2:00	
2:30	**SPENDING MONEY**
3:00	BUDGET / SPENT / REMAINING
3:30	
4:00	
4:30	**NOTES**
5:00	
5:30	

EAT

B	
L	
D	

AUSTRALIA BY VAN

TRAVEL DIARY

Date:

AUSTRALIA BY VAN

TRAVEL DIARY

Date:

SCHEDULE	SITESEEING
9:00	
9:30	
10:00	
10:30	
11:00	
11:30	
12:00	
12:30	**WEATHER**
1:00	
1:30	
2:00	
2:30	**SPENDING MONEY**
3:00	BUDGET / SPENT / REMAINING
3:30	
4:00	
4:30	**NOTES**
5:00	
5:30	

EAT

B	
L	
D	

AUSTRALIA BY VAN
TRAVEL DIARY

Date:

AUSTRALIA BY VAN

TRAVEL DIARY

Date:

SCHEDULE	SITESEEING
9:00	
9:30	
10:00	
10:30	
11:00	
11:30	
12:00	
12:30	**WEATHER**
1:00	
1:30	
2:00	
2:30	**SPENDING MONEY**
3:00	BUDGET · SPENT · REMAINING
3:30	
4:00	
4:30	**NOTES**
5:00	
5:30	

EAT

B	
L	
D	

AUSTRALIA BY VAN
TRAVEL DIARY

Date:

AUSTRALIA BY VAN

TRAVEL DIARY

Date:

SCHEDULE	SITESEEING
9:00	
9:30	
10:00	
10:30	
11:00	
11:30	
12:00	
12:30	**WEATHER**
1:00	
1:30	
2:00	
2:30	**SPENDING MONEY**
3:00	BUDGET / SPENT / REMAINING
3:30	
4:00	
4:30	**NOTES**
5:00	
5:30	

EAT

B	
L	
D	

AUSTRALIA BY VAN
TRAVEL DIARY

Date:

AUSTRALIA BY VAN

TRAVEL DIARY

Date:

SCHEDULE	SITESEEING
9:00	
9:30	
10:00	
10:30	
11:00	
11:30	
12:00	
12:30	WEATHER
1:00	
1:30	
2:00	
2:30	SPENDING MONEY
3:00	BUDGET / SPENT / REMAINING
3:30	
4:00	
4:30	NOTES
5:00	
5:30	

EAT

B

L

D

AUSTRALIA BY VAN
TRAVEL DIARY

Date:

AUSTRALIA BY VAN

TRAVEL DIARY

Date:

SCHEDULE	SITESEEING
9:00	
9:30	
10:00	
10:30	
11:00	
11:30	
12:00	
12:30	WEATHER
1:00	
1:30	
2:00	
2:30	SPENDING MONEY
3:00	
3:30	
4:00	
4:30	NOTES
5:00	
5:30	

SPENDING MONEY

BUDGET	SPENT	REMAINING

EAT

B	
L	
D	

AUSTRALIA BY VAN
TRAVEL DIARY

Date:

AUSTRALIA BY VAN

TRAVEL DIARY

Date:

SCHEDULE	SITESEEING
9:00	
9:30	
10:00	
10:30	
11:00	
11:30	
12:00	
12:30	WEATHER
1:00	
1:30	
2:00	
2:30	SPENDING MONEY
3:00	BUDGET · SPENT · REMAINING
3:30	
4:00	
4:30	NOTES
5:00	
5:30	

EAT

B	
L	
D	

AUSTRALIA BY VAN

TRAVEL DIARY

Date:

AUSTRALIA BY VAN

TRAVEL DIARY

Date:

SCHEDULE	SITESEEING
9:00	
9:30	
10:00	
10:30	
11:00	
11:30	
12:00	
12:30	**WEATHER**
1:00	
1:30	
2:00	
2:30	**SPENDING MONEY**
3:00	BUDGET / SPENT / REMAINING
3:30	
4:00	
4:30	**NOTES**
5:00	
5:30	

EAT

B	
L	
D	

AUSTRALIA BY VAN
TRAVEL DIARY

Date:

AUSTRALIA BY VAN
TRAVEL DIARY

Date:

SCHEDULE	SITESEEING
9:00	
9:30	
10:00	
10:30	
11:00	
11:30	
12:00	
12:30	WEATHER
1:00	
1:30	
2:00	
2:30	SPENDING MONEY

BUDGET	SPENT	REMAINING

| 3:00 |
| 3:30 |
| 4:00 |

NOTES

| 4:30 |
| 5:00 |
| 5:30 |

EAT

B	
L	
D	

AUSTRALIA BY VAN
TRAVEL DIARY

Date:

AUSTRALIA BY VAN

TRAVEL DIARY

Date:

SCHEDULE	SITESEEING
9:00	
9:30	
10:00	
10:30	
11:00	
11:30	
12:00	
12:30	**WEATHER**
1:00	
1:30	
2:00	
2:30	**SPENDING MONEY**
3:00	BUDGET / SPENT / REMAINING
3:30	
4:00	
4:30	**NOTES**
5:00	
5:30	

EAT

B	
L	
D	

AUSTRALIA BY VAN

TRAVEL DIARY

Date:

AUSTRALIA BY VAN

TRAVEL DIARY

Date:

SCHEDULE	SITESEEING
9:00	
9:30	
10:00	
10:30	
11:00	
11:30	
12:00	
12:30	**WEATHER**
1:00	
1:30	
2:00	
2:30	**SPENDING MONEY**
3:00	BUDGET / SPENT / REMAINING
3:30	
4:00	
4:30	**NOTES**
5:00	
5:30	

EAT

B	
L	
D	

AUSTRALIA BY VAN

TRAVEL DIARY

Date:

AUSTRALIA BY VAN
TRAVEL DIARY

Date:

SCHEDULE	SITESEEING
9:00	
9:30	
10:00	
10:30	
11:00	
11:30	
12:00	
12:30	**WEATHER**
1:00	
1:30	
2:00	
2:30	**SPENDING MONEY**
3:00	
3:30	
4:00	
4:30	**NOTES**
5:00	
5:30	

BUDGET	SPENT	REMAINING

EAT

B	
L	
D	

AUSTRALIA BY VAN
TRAVEL DIARY

Date:

AUSTRALIA BY VAN

TRAVEL DIARY

Date:

SCHEDULE	SITESEEING
9:00	
9:30	
10:00	
10:30	
11:00	
11:30	
12:00	
12:30	**WEATHER**
1:00	
1:30	
2:00	
2:30	**SPENDING MONEY**
3:00	
3:30	
4:00	
4:30	**NOTES**
5:00	
5:30	

SPENDING MONEY

BUDGET	SPENT	REMAINING

EAT

B	
L	
D	

AUSTRALIA BY VAN
TRAVEL DIARY

Date:

AUSTRALIA BY VAN

TRAVEL DIARY

Date:

SCHEDULE	SITESEEING
9:00	
9:30	
10:00	
10:30	
11:00	
11:30	
12:00	
12:30	WEATHER
1:00	
1:30	
2:00	
2:30	SPENDING MONEY

BUDGET	SPENT	REMAINING

SCHEDULE	
3:00	
3:30	
4:00	
4:30	NOTES
5:00	
5:30	

EAT

B	
L	
D	

AUSTRALIA BY VAN
TRAVEL DIARY

Date:

AUSTRALIA BY VAN

TRAVEL DIARY

Date:

SCHEDULE	SITESEEING
9:00	
9:30	
10:00	
10:30	
11:00	
11:30	
12:00	
12:30	WEATHER
1:00	
1:30	
2:00	
2:30	SPENDING MONEY
3:00	BUDGET / SPENT / REMAINING
3:30	
4:00	
4:30	NOTES
5:00	
5:30	

EAT

B	
L	
D	

AUSTRALIA BY VAN

TRAVEL DIARY

Date:

AUSTRALIA BY VAN

TRAVEL DIARY

Date:

SCHEDULE	SITESEEING
9:00	
9:30	
10:00	
10:30	
11:00	
11:30	
12:00	
12:30	**WEATHER**
1:00	
1:30	
2:00	
2:30	**SPENDING MONEY**
3:00	BUDGET / SPENT / REMAINING
3:30	
4:00	
4:30	**NOTES**
5:00	
5:30	

EAT

B	
L	
D	

AUSTRALIA BY VAN

TRAVEL DIARY

Date:

AUSTRALIA BY VAN

TRAVEL DIARY

Date:

SCHEDULE	SITESEEING
9:00	
9:30	
10:00	
10:30	
11:00	
11:30	
12:00	
12:30	**WEATHER**
1:00	
1:30	
2:00	
2:30	**SPENDING MONEY**

BUDGET	SPENT	REMAINING
3:00		
3:30		
4:00		

SCHEDULE	NOTES
4:30	
5:00	
5:30	

EAT

B	
L	
D	

AUSTRALIA BY VAN

TRAVEL DIARY

Date:

AUSTRALIA BY VAN

TRAVEL DIARY

Date:

SCHEDULE	SITESEEING
9:00	
9:30	
10:00	
10:30	
11:00	
11:30	
12:00	
12:30	**WEATHER**
1:00	
1:30	
2:00	
2:30	**SPENDING MONEY**

BUDGET	SPENT	REMAINING

SCHEDULE	
3:00	
3:30	
4:00	
4:30	**NOTES**
5:00	
5:30	

EAT

B	
L	
D	

AUSTRALIA BY VAN

TRAVEL DIARY

Date:

AUSTRALIA BY VAN

TRAVEL DIARY

Date:

SCHEDULE	SITESEEING
9:00	
9:30	
10:00	
10:30	
11:00	
11:30	
12:00	
12:30	**WEATHER**
1:00	
1:30	
2:00	
2:30	**SPENDING MONEY**
3:00	
3:30	
4:00	
4:30	**NOTES**
5:00	
5:30	

SPENDING MONEY		
BUDGET	SPENT	REMAINING

EAT

B	
L	
D	

AUSTRALIA BY VAN
TRAVEL DIARY

Date:

AUSTRALIA BY VAN

TRAVEL DIARY

Date:

SCHEDULE	SITESEEING
9:00	
9:30	
10:00	
10:30	
11:00	
11:30	
12:00	
12:30	**WEATHER**
1:00	
1:30	
2:00	
2:30	**SPENDING MONEY**
3:00	BUDGET · SPENT · REMAINING
3:30	
4:00	
4:30	**NOTES**
5:00	
5:30	

EAT

B	
L	
D	

WELCOME TO YOUR

TRAVEL
AUSTRALIA
BY VAN
PLANNER & DIARY

DIARY

Made in the USA
Columbia, SC
13 December 2021

51285514R00062